Games
Keyboarding
Teachers Play

This book is dedicated to keyboarding and typing teachers everywhere! For it is you who teach our students the most important computer skill they will ever learn—the ability to type!

Published by
TEACHING BUSINESS EDUCATION NEWSLETTER
P.O. Box 8558
Warwick, RI 02888
1-401-781-6921 Fax 1-401-781-7608
www.teachbused.com

GAMES KEYBOARDING TEACHERS PLAY
ISBN 0-9721331-0-0

Printed in the United States of America.

This book is available at quantity discounts for bulk purchases. For information, call 1-401-781-6921

Visit Teaching Business Education Newsletter on the Internet at http://www.teachbused.com

Credits: Grateful acknowledgements are made to Lisa Wardle and Monica Handy for their editorial expertise and support of this book.

GAMES
KEYBOARDING
TEACHERS
PLAY

A Collection of Creative Games,
Activities and Instructional
Strategies to Liven Any
Keyboarding Classroom

Michael Gecawich

Published by
Teaching Business Education Newsletter
Box 8558, Warwick, RI 02888
U.S.A.

FOREWORD

This book, *Games Keyboarding Teachers Play*, is a collection of sensational keyboarding teaching ideas drawn from the content of Teaching Business Education Newsletter. The newsletter was conceived in 1996 by nationally known editor and business educator Michael Gecawich. Teaching Business Education Newsletter is widely regarded as an energizing teaching idea resource for business educators. Many of the ideas you'll see in this book are drawn from top-notch keyboarding teachers from around the United States. So, you can rest assured they'll work for you in your own keyboarding classroom.

International superstar trainer and educator, Bob Pike, sums learning up best when he said "learning is directly proportional to the amount of fun you have." With that said, the goal of this book is to provide keyboarding and typing teachers with creative ideas and strategies that make teaching and learning how to keyboard a barrel of fun.

When integrated with your regular keyboarding curriculum, the ideas in this book are a surefire way to add zest and energy to your keyboarding classroom. You'll witness your students being more excited and enthusiastic about learning to keyboard. The end result will be more accurate, efficient and speedy keyboarders walking out the door at the end of your keyboarding course.

Enjoy the book!

Sincerely,
Michael Gecawich
Editor

DEDICATION

First and foremost, a huge thank you goes out to all of the outstanding teachers that contributed their keyboarding-teaching wizardry to this book. Your games, activities and strategies will help thousands of future keyboarding students to be the best they can be for many years to come.

This book would not be possible without the creativity and support of Lisa Wardle. Lisa's editorial expertise has helped make this book a down-to-earth, fun to read reference tool for keyboarding teachers.

And finally, to every keyboarding and typing teacher, active or retired, for your countless efforts in giving timed writing tests, dictation drills and coping with what sometimes can be a monotonous course to teach. The keyboarding skills you teach are like riding a bike, once learned, never forgotten. Thank you!

From the author:

To Kathy, Halle, Reis and Cass—you are my world.

To all of my family (especially Mom) and friends—thanks for being in my life.

INTRODUCTION

Before there were computers, the Internet, wireless mice and multimedia, there was the typewritter. A machine that once dominated the typewritten document world, has now found a place to settle collecting dust and cobwebs in garages, school storage closets and trash dumpsters. Yet, from this prehistoric invention, a skill was born that today remains unchanged. Of course, that skill is keyboarding.

The ability to type with swift speed and precision accuracy undoubtadley remains the most fundamental and important computer skill a person can possess.

The games, activities and strategies presented in this book will add a new dimension to how to teach and to how to learn keyboarding. One of the biggest challenges a keyboarding teacher faces is taking the day-to-day monotony out of learning how to type. Not to worry. The ideas in this book will spark new energy and spirit in your classroom. The games and activities have been carefully selected to offer students a variety of methods in which to learn. From snowflakes to fortune cookies, students will be creatively challenged to improve their keyboarding speed and accuracy skills.

So sit back in your teacher's desk and get ready to be inspired like you've never been before—here comes *Games Keyboarding Teachers Play*!

HOW TO USE THIS BOOK

The individual activities, games, and lessons in this book have been organized into six keyboarding instructional categories:

- Enrichment activities
- Keyboarding games
- Ideas that activate & motivate
- Bulletin boards that teach keyboarding
- Drill & practice activities
- Posture, technique & finger placement activities

A bonus section, titled *Keyboarding & Typing Internet Resource Directory*, is also included to provide keyboarding and typing teachers with a quick index to current Web sites that contain keyboarding related materials, articles, software and research.

For quick reading and easy-reference, each idea presented in this book is divided into the following checkpoints:

- Objective
- Procedure
- Materials Needed
- Time Required
- Contributor (If a contributor is not noted, either the source of the idea could not be found, or the idea is authored by the editors of Teaching Business Educaiton Newsletter).

With minor modifications, the ideas presented in this book can be easily adapted for any grade level. However, you will find that most of the activities are written for a secondary level student audience.

Note: Many of the ideas found in this book include Web site addresses that provide the reader with additional resource and reference material. When this book was printed, every effort was made to provide the reader with accurate Web site addresses.

CONTENTS

ENRICHMENT ACTIVITIES

KEYBOARDING GAMES

CONTENTS

ENRICHMENT
ACTIVITIES

CREATING 26 LETTER TIMING TESTS

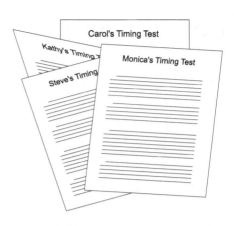

Objective:

To infuse variety into timed tests while also getting students to think creatively by having them use all 26 letters of the alphabet.

Procedure:

Challenge your keyboarding students with an activity that fosters their critical thinking skills. In this exercise, your students will be creating their own typing tests.

Here's how it works:

Explain to your students that they must create a paragraph that: (a) uses all 26 letters of the alphabet; (b) makes sense; and (c) conveys a short story.

Next, have the students calculate the number of words on each line and the total number of words in the paragraph. Have them use a format similar to that included in standard keyboarding textbooks.

Explain to your students that these paragraphs will be used for future timed writings. This will encourage them to stay focused and improve their performances.

Collect the best ones and save them for future use in all your keyboarding classes.

Materials Needed:

Computer, plain sheets of paper and a printer.

Time Required:

Approximately one class period.

CREATIVE MANUSCRIPTING

Objectives:
To provide students with interesting material to keyboard.
To provide practice for students in formatting manuscripts.

Procedure:

Note: The students need to have completed one unit on manuscript typing prior to starting this exercise.

Here's how it works:

1. Using current periodicals such as <u>Newsweek</u>, cut out one-page articles on various topics (science, environment, life-styles, business, etc.), mount them on colored paper and laminate each one (optional).

2. Let each student select one article that interests him.

3. Tell your students that they may decide whether to type an unbound, left or top bound manuscript based on the article selected.

4. Instruct your students to type the article verbatim except that they must, somewhere in the document, add one original sentence. This forces students to read and understand what the article is all about. For ease in locating the added sentence, instruct your students to underline or boldface it.

Material Needed:
A variety of magazine and newspaper articles, colored paper and a laminating machine (optional).

Time Required:
Approximately one class period.

Contributor:
Sue Lyons, CBE Coordinator, Mogadore High School, Mogadore, OH

YOUR SCHOOL TRIVIA CHALLENGE

Objective:
To challenge teams of students to type answers to school-related trivia questions in a competitive fashion.

Procedure:

Challenge your students to be the wisest owl and the fastest typist in the class by answering school-related trivia questions.

Some possible trivia questions you can use:

- What is the date our school was opened?
- What is the name of our school's principal(s)?
- What is the name of our school's assistant principal(s)?
- What is our school motto?
- What is our school song?
- Who is the head baseball coach?
- Who teaches economics?
- What is the time of our school's starting bell?
- What is the time of the ending bell?

Here's how it works:

Divide the class into groups of four students each. Set the timer for a pre-determined time frame.

Using the trivia questions handout created prior to beginning the game, have the group type their responses.

The first group to hand in its responses typed properly with the most correct answers wins the game. Award prizes to the top three finishers.

Materials Needed:
A teacher-created handout of school-related trivia questions and small prizes (optional).

4

Time Required:

Approximately one class period.

Contributor:

Janice Shuffield, Business Teacher, Marcus High School, Flower Mound, TX

FOR THE EARLY FINISHERS

Objectives:
To provide enrichment practice for students who
complete assigned work early.

Procedure:

Every classroom has its speedy typists—the students who finish their typing
drills earlier than the others in the class. This is an ideal activity for those
students as it provides an opportunity for them to improve on their composing
skills. Additionally, it can be used throughout the term as an ongoing source of
extra credit, thus motivating students to complete their daily class work.

Keep file folders in your classroom that are chocked-full of fun and
constructive typing assignments. Some suggestions: brainteasers, grammar
confusers, story starters, Internet assignments, etc.

Number code each assignment in order to provide both student and
teacher a mechanism that keeps track of completed assignments.

At the end of the marking period, provide extra-credit to students who
have completed the additional activities.

Materials Needed:
Supplemental written materials such as: puzzles, newspaper articles, and
brainteasers.

Time Required:
Use throughout a keyboarding or typing course.

Contributor:
Mary Lou Vaniels, Cave Spring Jr. High School, Roanoke, VA

SPORTS TEAM LETTERS GET STUDENTS EXCITED

Objective:
To teach students how to format a business letter and an envelope.

Procedure:

Most teachers are met with a less than enthusiastic response when they instruct their students to set up a business letter and envelope. However, when the project gets the students involved and gives them a payoff in the form of return mail, the dynamics change.

Here's how it works:

Have your students obtain the mailing address of their favorite professional sports team.

Instruct students to formulate a business letter that requests a team photo, bumper sticker and other promotional items. Most teams are more than willing to accommodate the request.

Next, have students format a business sized envelope. They must proof-read the letters carefully and then mail them away.

Materials Needed:
A copy of The Kid's Address Book by Michael Levine (ISBN 0-399-52304), one envelope and a stamp for each student participating in the activity.

Time Required:
Approximately one class period.

Contributor:
Darlene Martin, Computer Teacher, Highland Middle School, Beaver Falls, PA

SONG LYRICS BREAK UP THE MONOTONY

Objective:
To provide students with a break from keyboarding textbook drills.

Procedure:

Sometimes it can be monotonous for students to continually key in assignments from word processing or keyboarding textbooks. To break up the routine in keyboarding or word processing classes, have your students type the lyrics of popular songs.

Here's how it works:

1. Obtain copies of a variety of song lyrics and then pass them out to your students. You can find a host of downloadable song lyrics online at **http://www.lyricsworld.com/**. This Web site contains a searchable database that provides the lyrics to thousands of popular songs.

2. Instruct the students to key in the lyrics.

3. Have your students print their songs and compare them for accuracy to the original song.

Materials Needed:
A variety of song lyrics printed out and then provided to students as handouts.

Time Required:
Approximately one class period.

Contributor:
Larry Luehrs, Business Technology Teacher, Kahuku High School, Kahuku, HI

ADOPT A TYPING STUDENT

Objective:
To give real-world keyboarding experience to students by having them perform clerical tasks for school staff members.

Procedure:

Adopting a typing student is a great way to help students gain some real-life work experience within a school.

Here's how to get the program up and running in your school:

1. Conduct a survey among the teachers in your school to determine who would be interested in receiving typing services offered by your students. It will come as no surprise that the teachers respond very favorably to the offer.

2. Distribute a form to all interested teachers with an explanation of the project and their part in the evaluation process. The form must contain a section that requires the teacher to specify the time period (anywhere from one week to four weeks) that the teacher will be needing the student's services.

3. During a four week period one class a week is devoted to having the students perform the various jobs for the teachers to whom they are assigned. The amount of time spent each week on this project can be adjusted depending upon the needs of your class.

4. At the completion of each word period, the student takes an evaluation form to his respective teacher to be filled out and returned to you. This form serves as the student's grade for that day.

5. Discuss the evaluation form with the student prior to beginning the next week's assignment.

Our contributor, Diann Dodd, reports that "the results are great, and the teachers love having an assistant. The students also enjoy the experience— they realize the importance of performing a job correctly."

Materials Needed:

No additional materials required.

Time Required:

Teacher's discretion.

Contributor:

Diann Dodd, Business Teacher & Department Head, Catoosa High School, Catoosa, OK

THE HUMAN SCAVENGER HUNT

Objectives:
To provide students an opportunity to interact with one another thereby getting to know each other better.
To infuse variety into keyboarding practice.

Procedure:

After students have learned all the letter keys, send them on a human scavenger hunt. Your students will not only have a lot of fun with the activity but also will learn something new about their fellow classmates.

Here's how it works:

1. Distribute to each student the list you prepared regarding the information they must find out about each other. Use your imagination—the questions are endless.
   Some examples are:
   • Find someone who has a birthday in the same month as you.
   • Find someone who likes to downhill ski.
   • Find someone who walks to school.

   To foster interaction among all students, the same name can only appear twice on the student's scavenger hunt sheet.

2. When the students have answers to all twenty-five questions, they must return to their keyboards and type in the first and last names of the students who correspond with each question.

3. Students then print out their list of names. To add a competitive touch to the activity, challenge students to see who can finish the scavenger hunt the fastest. The top-three finishers can be rewarded with a small prize such as a candy bar.

Variation: For more keying practice, have students key in the questions, responses and student names.

11

Materials Needed:

A prepared list of twenty-five items that students are required to find out about each other. A small prize (optional).

Time Required:

Approximately one or two class periods.

Contributor:

Julie Pasowicz, Bay Port High School, Howard-Suamico School District, Green Bay, WI

GET 'EM COOKING

Objective:
To provide an opportunity for students to utilize and practice their keyboarding skills by producing a collection of recipes that eventually becomes a cookbook.

Procedure:

Get your students' keyboarding skills "sizzling" by having them create a cookbook.

Here's how it works:
1. Start by having your students bring in recipes in the following categories:
   - Appetizers
   - Breads
   - Desserts
   - Entrees

The recipes can be obtained from magazines, newspapers (specifically the food section), cereal boxes, cookbooks and Web sites (visit **www.cooking.com** and **www.yumyum.com**).

2. Organize and label the recipes into their respective categories (appetizers, breads, desserts and entrees).

3. Divide the class into groups. Have each group key in an assigned recipe category. Provide students with formatting guideline such as font choice, page margins, etc.

4. Once the students have completed keying in all the recipes, have them design a creative cookbook cover page.

5. Next, have students collect copies of the typed recipes from their fellow classmates. Bind the recipes by using a three whole punch and yarn, or staples. Alternatively, the completed recipe book can be placed in a clear vinyl presentation folder.

Idea: Students can give the recipe books as a gift for Mother's Day or any other occasion.

Materials Needed:
A variety of recipes.

Time Required:
Approximately two weeks.

Contributor:
Brenda Humphries, Business Department Chairperson and Teacher, Rock Hill High School, Rock Hill, SC

PROOFREADER'S PICTURES

Objective:
To teach and reinforce the use of proofreading marks.

Procedure:

After introducing proofreader marks to students, have them create a picture using any or all of the proofreader marks (see the sample illustration provided on the next page).

You can download a complete set of proofreader's marks at Internet address **http://www.espressographics.com/text/proofreader.html**.

Materials Needed:
Handouts of proofreader marks and symbols.

Time Required:
One class period.

Contributor:
Sandra Dunbar, Brick Township Memorial High School, Brick, NJ

Sample proofreader marks drawing:

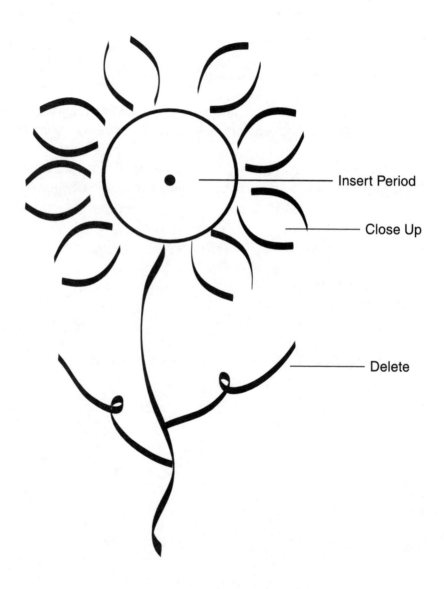

Insert Period

Close Up

Delete

LITTLE PICTURES, BIG STORIES

Objective:
To provide secondary level students with an opportunity to collaborate with elementary school students in a creative exercise that enhances the older students' writing and keyboarding skills.

Procedure:

Give your keyboarding students a chance to make a child's day.

Here's how it works:

Ask an elementary teacher in your school district to have his students draw a picture that will be sent to your high school keyboarding students (children in grades K-2 are the optimum age group for this exercise). Be sure to have enough pictures so that each keyboarding student receives at least one.

Upon receipt of the pictures, have your keyboarding students write a story for the pictures they received. Assign one picture per student. Before students begin writing and keying in stories, be sure to specify the length and any formatting guidelines. Have students proofread their work carefully.

When the stories are complete, send them back to the elementary students. The elementary students will love the attention from the "big kids," while the upper level students gain practice in their writing and keyboarding skills while bringing joy to a "little kid."

Materials Needed:
Not applicable.

Time Required:
Teacher's discretion, depending upon the frequency desired.

Contributor:
Jeff Hall, Business Teacher, Ridewood High School,
New Port Richey, FL

CHRISTMAS KEYBOARDING PROJECT

Objectives:
To provide students with a hands-on experience in writing and typing response letters.
To enhance the ability of students to work under pressure in order to meet a deadline.
To create interdepartmental and interschool relations that benefits all involved. This is a "feel-good" project that not only teaches but also engenders goodwill within the community.

Procedure:

At the beginning of the school year explain to your students that they will be acting as Santa's helpers by responding to the letters the local elementary school children write to Santa. Your students will be responsible for composing and sending return letters to these children. Inform them that in order to participate in this project, they will need to master typing a business letter and an envelope by the end of November.

During the Christmas season, students from the local elementary schools (this can be broadened to a larger area, if desired) write letters to Santa. Their teachers collect this "mail" and forward it via interschool mail to the participating keyboarding classes.

The resources and talents of various groups within your school will be utilized. The Arts and Graphics departments are responsible for designing the Santa stationery. The English and Business departments are responsible for composing the return letters from Santa. This group effort ensures that every child receives a personal letter from Santa.

Our contributor, Jeanne Ryan, of Westfield, Massachusetts, writes enthusiastically of her school's success. "Once the project is known, letters from former city residents who live as far away as California and Florida are sent to the school for personalized answers." She goes on to say, "Many of these students remember the excitement of receiving their own letters when they were little children themselves, and that memory gives them the motivation to type as many letters as they possibly can." Ryan notes that over 1,500 letters to Santa are answered in just a two-week period.

Variation: If desired, the local post office can also be enlisted to help. Any "letters to Santa" that arrive at the post office can be directed to the Business department for inclusion in the project.

Note: Prior to conducting this project, seek approval from your school administrator.

Materials Needed:
Computer and printer.

Time Required:
This is a long-term project that ideally begins at the start of the school year and extends until the week before Christmas vacation.

Contributor:
Jeanne Ryan, Business Educator, Westfield High School, Westfield, MA

THE TWELVE DAYS OF CHRISTMAS

Objectives:
To provide students with practice in keyboarding and use of the "copy" and "paste" feature.

Procedure:

Bring holiday cheer into your keyboarding classroom with the song "Twelve Days of Christmas."

Here's how it works:
Have your students key the first and second lines of the song Twelve Days of Christmas.

On the first day of Christmas my true love sent to me
A partridge in a pear tree

Have students' copy and paste the first two lines and insert "Two turtle doves" between them. Also change the word "first" to "second" in the first line.

On the <u>second</u> day of Christmas my true love sent to me
Two turtle doves <insert>
And a partridge in a pear tree

Have students' copy and paste the first three lines and insert "Three French hens" after the first line. Change the word "second" to "third" in the first line. See below.

On the <u>third</u> day of Christmas my true love sent to me
Three French hens <insert>
Two turtle doves
And a partridge in a pear tree

Repeat this same procedure until all 12 verses are completed. Have students print the song.

Variation: Have students add clipart to enhance their documents.

Materials Needed:
Copies of the song "Twelve Days of Christmas" or an equivalent non denominational song if religious sensitivity is an issue. Suggested alternative: the folk song "There Was an Old Lady Who Swallowed a Fly."

Time Required:
Approximately 30-40 minutes.

Contributor:
Carol Conover, Business Education Department Head, Grafton High School, Grafton, WI

SELF-ESTEEM KEYBOARDING

Objective:
To give students practice in composing sentences that helps boost their self-esteem.

Procedure:

Ask each student in your class to key one positive statement about each other. In order to avoid any inappropriate comments, instruct the students that statements regarding the physical attributes of other students are not allowed.

Students should put the name of the student they are typing about before each positive statement. For instance, a student might key; *Janice is a great basketball player.* Students should double space between each statement.

Have each student print their comments, cut out each individual statement and deliver them to each student. *Note: You may want to review the comments for appropriate content before distributing them.*

Your students will get some extra keyboarding practice and will leave your class wearing a big smile for the day!

Materials Needed:
No special materials required.

Time Required:
Approximately 30-40 minutes.

Contributor:
Mrs. Sharon B. Sowers, Teacher, George Wythe High School, Wytheville, VA

NEW LETTER TRIVIA

Objective:
To have some fun while reviewing new letters your students have learned.

Procedure:

Add some fun to the end of your lessons that introduce new letter keys by asking your students to key the answers to trivia questions (a list of between ten to twenty questions is sufficient). The key to the activity is that all the answers start with the new letter(s) introduced that given day.

Here's an example if the letter "I" is being introduced:

What company manufacturers over 90 percent of the micro-processing chips used in computers?

Answer: Intel

Materials Needed:
A list of ten to twenty trivia questions that are created by the teacher.

Time Required:
Approximately 4-5 minutes.

Contributor:
Tory Klementsen, MCP, Business and Technology Educator, Marysville Pilchuck High School, Marysville, WA

ACROMANIA

```
ASAP
CPA
FBI
IRS
RDA
OSHA
TBA
```

Objective:
To teach and reinforce the proper use of the
CAPS LOCK key.

Procedure:

To teach students to use the CAPS LOCK key, employ the use of acronyms.
Since the majority of acronyms are capitalized, they lend themselves nicely to
teaching the use of the CAPS LOCK key.

Here's how it works:

Have students type from a teacher prepared list of acronyms. For additional keying practice, have students try to key in the meaning of each acronym.

You can quickly create your list of acronyms by visiting the Acronym
Finder Web site at **http://www.acronymfinder.com/**.

Materials Needed:
A list, prepared by the teacher, that contains a variety of acronyms.

Time Required:
Approximately one class period.

Contributor:
Tory Klementsen, MCP, Business and Technology Educator,
Marysville Pilchuck High School, Marysville, WA

10 YEARS FROM NOW...

Objective:
To give students practice in keyboarding while alternatively exercising their creative writing skills.

Procedure:

To enhance keyboarding practices while exercising students' creative writing skills, have them write and type a one page paper on the following topic:

> "Write to me (the teacher) as if it were ten years from now. Tell me where you are, what you are doing and how you got there."

Materials Needed:
No additional materials required.

Time Required:
Approximately one class period.

Contributor:
Tory Klementsen, MCP, Business and Technology Educator, Marysville Pilchuck High School, Marysville, WA

LETTERS TO SOMEONE YOU ADMIRE

Objective:
To give students practice in both keyboarding and
writing techniques.

Procedure:

Get a copy of Michael Levine's <u>The Kid's Address Book</u> (ISBN:
0399526889 Publisher: Berkley Publishing Group) from your local bookstore
or library. The book, geared towards kids, informs them how and where they
can contact the coolest names in Hollywood, the most important politicians
and the most exciting organizations and clubs. Both postal addresses and e-
mail addresses are included in the book.

Some of the popular choices included in the book are: N'Sync, Britney
Spears, Jim Carrey, Shaquille O'Neill, Leonardo Di Caprio, Rosie
O'Donnell, Mark McGwire, Greenpeace, Will Smith, Eminem, Gwyneth
Paltrow, Melissa Joan Hart, and many more!

You can also access thousands of celebrity addresses online at *The Star
Archive* Web site at **http://www.stararchive.com**.

To give students practice in keyboarding and writing a personal business
letter, have them select one person to write to from the book. Who knows,
they might even get a reply!

Materials Needed:
<u>The Kid's Address Book</u> by Michael Levine ISBN: 0399526889 Publisher:
Berkley Publishing Group.

Time Required:
Approximately one class period.

Contributor:
Tory Klementsen, MCP, Marysville Pilchuck High School, Business and
Technology Educator, Marysville, WA

ALPHABET SOUP KEYBOARDING

Objective:
To provide students with a fun activity that allows them to key sentences that use every letter of the alphabet.

Procedure:

Ask students to create an alphabetical listing that refers to something meaningful or of interest to them.

Students type the first letter of each section in parenthesis and then type the sentence or phrase that goes with it.

The following topics are suggested: friends, family, school, and summer. Other topics can be allowed upon your prior approval.

The document should be formatted using a title with no more than one line per letter allowed.

An example is provided on the next page.

Materials Needed:
No special materials required.

Time Required:
Approximately one class period.

Contributor:
Tonya D. Skinner, Business Education Department, Oran High School, Oran, MO

Example of alphabet soup keyboarding:

Topic: A Friend

(A)ccepts you as you are
(B)elieves in "you"
(C)alls you just to say "HI"
(D)oesn't give up on you
(E)nvisions the whole of you (even the unfinished parts)
(F)orgives your mistakes
(G)ives unconditionally
(H)elps you
(I)nvites you over
(J)ust hangs out with you
(K)eeps you close at heart
(L)oves you for who you are
(M)akes a difference in your life
(N)ever judges
(O)ffers support
(P)icks you up
(Q)uiets your fears
(R)aises your spirits
(S)ays nice things about you
(T)ells you the truth when you need to hear it
(U)nderstands you
(V)alues you
(W)alks beside you
(X)-plains things you don't understand
(Y)ells when you won't listen and
(Z)aps you back to reality

THINK OR SINK

Objective:
This game will help students compose original documents that require critical thinking.

Procedure:

If students finish their assigned work early, have them compose a *Think or Sink* essay. *Think or Sink* topics challenge students to use their critical thinking and creative writing skills.

Essays should be written in the student's own words with no outside assistance (other people, internet, etc.) and must be proofread before they are printed.

Sample *Think or Sink* essay topics:

- List ten things your class could do to help the homeless.
- A new law has been passed to outlaw television. You must live by the law.
- List ten things you would do instead of watching television.
- If you could add one day to every week, what would you name that day? Explain your reasoning.
- If I walked into your room right now, what would it look like?
- You are interviewing your hero but can ask him or her only five questions. What would you ask?
- Describe a recent meal without including the names of any foods or drinks.
- A genie has just told you that you can trade places with anyone in the world for an hour. Who would you absolutely not want to trade places with? Why?
- If you could read your teacher's mind, what do you think it would say?
- You don't have any money but would like to give your mother (or father) a special birthday present. What will you do?

• If the teacher left you in charge of the class for an entire week, how would you plan your week? You will be observed and evaluated just as a teacher is, so no goofing off!

• A new law has been passed that raises the driving age to 35 years old, the age of the safest drivers according to the Insurance Association. Write a persuasive speech to convince the lawmakers that someone younger should be allowed to drive.

• Pretend that you are a parent talking to a child. Explain ten things that you would want that child to know about life.

• You are attending the UFO convention. You are the keynote speaker and must prepare a speech entitled "UFO's—Fact or Fiction." Write this speech.

• If you were governor of a state that bordered an ocean, what would you do to protect the ocean from pollution?

Variations: Allow students to come up with their own *Think or Sink* topics.

Material Needed:
A handout that you create that uses some or all of the "Think or Sink" questions provided.

Time Required:
Variable, dependent upon teacher's discretion.

Contributor:
Tonya D. Skinner, Business Education Department, Oran High School, Oran, MO

PASS YOUR FORTUNE

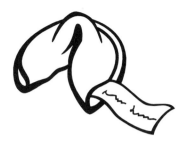

Objectives:
To give students practice in keyboarding sentences.
To add variety and fun to a keyboarding course.

Procedure:

This activity will fill your keyboarding class with chuckles and lots of keyboarding energy.

Here's how it works:
1. Give each student in your class a fortune cookie.
2. Have students crack open their cookie and remove the fortune inside.
3. Students write their name on the back of their fortune paper.
4. Have students key in their fortune message along with their name next to it.
5. The fortune is then passed on to the next student to key in.
6. The fortunes are passed around the class for each student to type until every student receives his or her original fortune.
7. When all fortunes are keyed in, select one or two students to read the fortunes and the accompanying names to the rest of the class. The students will enjoy listening to the funny and sometimes outrageous fortunes.

Material Needed:
One fortune cookie for each student in the class.

Time Required:
Approximately 25 minutes.

KEYBOARDING
GAMES

KEYBOARDING HANGMAN

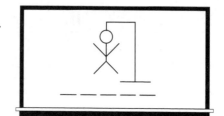

Objectives:
To provide students with practice in
remembering proper finger placement on
the keyboard.
Also serves as an excellent reinforcement activity.

Procedure:

Keyboarding hangman takes its name from the familiar guessing game "Hangman." It facilitates the student's remembering which finger corresponds to which letter on the keyboard.

Here's how to play:
    Keyboarding hangman is played in the same manner as traditional hangman with the following addition: when a student gives a letter to be used in the puzzle, he must also say what finger strikes that letter. Example: If Joshua wants to guess the letter Q, he would say "Q, left pinkie," or if Tiffany wants to guess the letter M, she would say "M, right pointer finger." Don't forget to establish what body parts are needed to complete the "man" prior to starting the game.
    Keyboarding hangman offers a fun alternative to a regular typing lesson and serves as a very effective finger placement reinforcement activity.

Materials Needed:
Chalkboard.

Time Required:
One fifty minute class period.

Contributor:
Kathleen Cornelison, Business Educator, Jefferson Middle School,
Jefferson, WI

TYPING SCATTERGORIES ®

Objective:
To develop keyboarding speed, accuracy, formatting and quick thinking skills.

Procedure:

Try this game to add some excitement to your keyboarding or typing classes. If you've played the popular Milton Bradley® board game Scattergories®, you'll quickly catch on. The game reinforces quick and accurate typing skills.

Here's how to play:
Before class begins, write down five categories that are relevant to your students (e.g., sports, items found in a locker, movies, TV shows, famous actors, etc.).
Begin the game by putting one category on the board. With timer in hand, call out one letter from the alphabet and say "go." A one-minute time limit is given for each category.
Students must quickly type a list of words that start with the designated letter and relate to the given category. If, for instance, you had designated the letter "F" for the category of sports, some of the responses might be: football, field hockey, and fencing.

Keeping score: After each one-minute round, you call on the students, asking them to list their responses for each category. If no one else in the class has listed a duplicate response, a point is awarded to that student. The student with the most points at the end of five rounds is declared the winner.

Materials Needed:
List of categories for use in the Scattergories® game, a stopwatch or one-minute timer.

Time Required:
Approximately one class period.

TEAM KEYBOARDING

Objective:
To let students have fun working in a team environment while stressing the importance of typing accuracy and speed.

Procedure:

Turn your keyboarding class into an exciting keyboarding competition by playing team keyboarding.

Here's how to play:
1. Divide your students into groups of four.
2. Provide each group with the text you have preselected.
3. Inform the groups that each student in the group will be typing for one minute each.
4. Using a timer, start the first student in each group. Stop after one minute has elapsed.
5. Then, the next student gets ready to start where the previous student finished. Start the timer for the second student.
6. The process continues until all four students have typed. If there are only three students in a group, have one of the three type twice.
7. The students print and circle their errors.

Keeping score: The group that types the furthest and has the least number of errors wins. Candy can be given to the winning team.

Variation: Same as above but don't stop the timer when the students change.

Materials Needed:
One computer or typewriter for every group of four students, candy (optional), timer, typing textbook or article of text that contains at least one page of appropriate typing material.

Time Required:

One class period.

Contributor:

Janice Shuffield, Business Teacher, Marcus High School, Flower Mound, TX

TYPING BOGGLE

Objective:
To reinforce typing skills by playing a
competitive friendly game that should be
familiar to most students.

Procedure:

Take a break from your daily classroom typing routine with this fun activity.
It's called *Typing Boggle*, adapted from the popular board game Boggle® by
Parker Brothers®. To play Typing Boggle, students use a matrix of letters to
think up and type as many words as possible in a given period of time.

Here's how to play:
  1. Using an overhead transparency or the chalkboard, draw a square.
  2. Divide the square into sixteen equal squares (4 lines vertically and 4
lines horizontally: see illustration provided).
  3. Fill each cube with a letter (be sure to use plenty of vowels.) Instruct
students <u>not</u> to copy the matrix drawn.
  4. Set a timer or stop watch for 5 minutes.
  5. From the jumbled letters, instruct the students to type as many words as
possible in the given time frame.
  6. When the time expires, the student(s) with the most words wins.

Materials Needed:
A matrix drawing as shown in the illustration provided.

Time Required:
Approximately one class period.

Contributor:
Sharon Watkins, Typing Teacher, Twin Creeks Middle School, Spring, TX

Sample Typing Boggle Matrix

A	T	C	E
B	O	S	I
U	D	L	Y
P	G	F	H

BASKETBALL & BASEBALL KEYBOARDING

Objective:
To use the game of basketball or baseball to enhance keyboarding skills.

Procedure:

Adapt the game of basketball to motivate keyboarding students to excel in their typing speeds. The faster a student types, the more points he scores for his team.

Here's how to play:

1. Divide your class into two equal teams.

2. Then, depending on what is appropriate for your class, have the students complete a 2, 3, or 5-minute timed writing.

3. As in the real game of basketball, there are only three ways to score points (regular shot, three-point shot and a foul shot). Set your point total equivalents for the class based on the speeds the students are capable of achieving.

For example:

If a student achieves a typing score between 15 to 20 wpm, his team is awarded 1 point (foul shot).

If a student achieves a typing score between 21 to 29 wpm, his team is awarded 2 points (regular shot).

If a student achieves a typing score equal to or greater than 30 wpm, his team is awarded 3 points (three point shot).

Note: Adjust the type speed range and point equivalents based on the skill level of your class.

4. Upon completion of the timed writing, go to each team member and add his score to the team total. Another option is to have them indicate by a show of hands how many had one point, two points, and so on.

5. Record the team totals four times to represent the four quarters played in the real game of basketball.

Baseball Keyboarding:

The same game can also be played using a baseball theme. One point equals a single, two points equals a double, three points equals a triple, and four points qualify as a home run. As you go up and down the aisles, you must figure out how many runs have been scored by each team. Anyone that doesn't maintain the minimum speed is an automatic out. Three outs end that team's at bat. Once the teams have run through their entire lineup, the team with the most runs scored wins.

Additional Variations: This game can really become a fun and lively contest by adding your own little gimmicks. Encourage the students to select teams' names, players' names, etc.

To discourage disruptive behavior, inform the students that you are the referee with fouls called and points deducted for each foul.

Materials Needed:
No special materials required.

Time Required:
Teacher's discretion.

Contributor:
Dom Annunziata, Wayne, NJ

THE GREAT 50 STATES CHALLENGE

Objective:
To add some competitive fun to your keyboarding class by challenging students to type all fifty states.

Procedure:

Add some fun to your keyboarding classes by presenting students with a competition: Who can be the first to type all fifty states?

Here's how to play:

1. Distribute copies of a handout containing the names of all fifty states.

2. Challenge students to compete against each other to see who can type the names of the fifty states the fastest and most accurately.

3. The student who finishes typing the list first is the winner.
Note: The number of errors should be calculated in the evaluation process.

4. Prizes can be awarded to the top three finishers. These prizes should reflect the theme of the competition, such as a certificate (made on the computer) that includes a graphic of a trophy and a map of the United States.

Variation: This activity also works well using the names of the presidents of the United States or the fifty capital cities.

Materials Needed:
A handout which contains the names of all fifty states. A reproducible handout is provided on the next page.

Time Required:
Approximately 15-20 minutes.

The 50 U.S. States

Alabama	Montana
Alaska	Nebraska
Arizona	Nevada
Arkansas	New Hampshire
California	New Jersey
Colorado	New Mexico
Connecticut	New York
Delaware	North Carolina
Florida	North Dakota
Georgia	Ohio
Hawaii	Oklahoma
Idaho	Oregon
Illinois	Pennsylvania
Indiana	Rhode Island
Iowa	South Carolina
Kansas	South Dakota
Kentucky	Tennessee
Louisiana	Texas
Maine	Utah
Maryland	Vermont
Massachusetts	Virginia
Michigan	Washington
Minnesota	West Virginia
Mississippi	Wisconsin
Missouri	Wyoming

TYPE-OFF CONTEST RAISES AWARENESS AND FUNDS

Objective:
To promote keyboarding throughout the school while raising money for a good cause.

Procedure:

If you're looking to earn extra-funds for a good cause, try establishing this "Type-Off Contest." The funds it generates can be used to support a business scholarship that honors the memory of a past business education teacher or any other worthwhile endeavor.

Here's how it works:

1. Each keyboarding student solicits sponsors who pledge to pay a certain amount of money for the average number of words-per-minute achieved by the student in the contest.

Example: a donation of ten cents a word would generate $4.00 for a student who keys 40 NWPM (40 NWPM x 10 cents=$4.00).

2. As an incentive, prizes are given to those students generating the most income (i.e., either through their spectacular typing speed, or alternatively for the slower typists who were able to generate the most sponsors). There are winners all around!

3. The top competitors are honored with trophies for a variety of categories including: highest average words-per-minute, most sponsors, most funds raised, etc.

Students are motivated to key faster, solicit sponsors, and bring in the most cash for a worthwhile cause.

44

Materials Needed:
Fundraising forms, small prizes and trophies.

Time Required:
Teacher's discretion.

Contributor:
Teri Principe, Business Education Department Chair,
Red Bank Catholic High School, Red Bank, NJ

PLAY "TYPING OUTBURST"

Objective:
To improve keyboarding speed and accuracy skills.

Procedure:

To help motivate students and promote quick typing and thinking skills, use an adaptation from the popular Parker Brothers® board game Outburst® in your keyboarding classes. Either version of the game (child or adult) works well.

Here's how to play:

    1. Divide the class into small teams (optional).

    2. Using the Outburst® game cards and a timer, call out the given category.

    3. Students have the allotted time to type as many answers as they can until the time runs out.

    4. Play as many rounds as desired.

The team with the most correct answers wins!

Materials Needed:
The board game Outburst® by Parker Brothers®.

Time Required:
Teacher's discretion.

Contributor:
Carol Enlow, Business Teacher, Heath High School, W. Paducah, KY

KEYBOARDING FOOTBALL

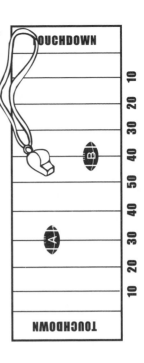

Objective:
To inject some competitive fun into a keyboarding class while reinforcing speed and accurate keyboarding skills.

Procedure:

Use the popular sport of football to boost the energy level of your keyboarding students.

Here's how to play:

1. Divide the class into two equal teams. As you set up the teams, give thought to balancing the groups to ensure an equal skill level on each side. You want to avoid having your fastest typers on the same team. Have each team select a captain. The captain is responsible for reporting her team's score to the teacher.

2. Draw a football field on the board and mark the end zones with the name of each team. Stick a laminated football to the board using a piece of masking tape.

3. Select appropriate short timed-writings and distribute copies to each student.

4. The game begins by administering a short timed-writing test to each team. The suggested timing test is 30-45 seconds. It works well and keeps the game moving rapidly. To add some reality to the game, use a coach's whistle to start and end each timed-writing.

5. After the completion of each timed-writing test, each student counts up the total number of correct words typed during the allotted time. The team captain is then responsible to add up the total number of words typed by all of her teammates and reports the total to the teacher.

6. Compare the total words typed by the two teams. Subtract the total number of words typed by the lower team from the higher team's total. The difference is how many yards toward the opposing team's end zone the ball is

47

moved. For example, if team A typed a total of 100 words and team B typed 90 words, the ball would move 10 yards toward team B's end zone.

7. When a team scores a touchdown, that team earns 7 points and the ball returns to the 50-yard line to begin a new round.

The team with the highest number of points within the given timeframe wins!

Variation: Sprinkle some humor on to the game by using bright yellow cards or hanker chiefs as penalty flags. Penalties can be issued following these guidelines:

- Illegal use of the eyes (looking at the keyboard) is a 10 yard penalty
- Illegal procedure (typing before the instructor says "go") is a 10 yard penalty
- Illegal use of hands (using the wrong finger) is a 10 yard penalty

Materials Needed:
Chalkboard or whiteboard, a laminated football (optional), masking tape, short timed-writing paragraphs, and a coaching whistle (optional).

Time Required:
One class period.

Contributor:
Scott Christy, Business Instructor, Green Bay East High School, Green Bay, WI

KEYBOARDING TRACK MEET

Objective:

To give students an opportunity to compete, as teams, while practicing speed, endurance and capitalization skills.

Procedure:

Here's a great game that simulates a real track and field competition in the keyboarding classroom.

Here's how to play:

Divide the class into teams consisting of 4-6 members each. As you set up the teams, give thought to balancing the groups to ensure an equal skill level on each side. If there is an unequal number of members on one team, some players will have to go twice during the game.

Game rules: Points for each track event are awarded based on how many teams you have. If you have 4 teams participating, for instance, the first place team for an event receives 4 points, the second place team receives 3 points and so on. To keep the game from being a one-sided mismatch, each team can receive only one set of points for each event. For example, if a person on team A places first and another person on team A places second in the same event, team A cannot receive the point value for both first and second place. In this case, team A receives the point value for first place only. Second place points would be rewarded to the next closest team finishing behind team A.

The events for the keyboarding track meet are as follows:

• **Sprints:** The first person on a team to correctly type a complete given line is awarded first place. The second finisher from another team is awarded second place and so on.

• **Distance:** Using a long paragraph (equivalent to a typical 3-5 minute timed-writing paragraph), the first person to correctly type the entire paragraph wins the points for the team. Second place is awarded to the team that finishes the paragraph second. Third place points are awarded to the team that completes it third and so on.

• **Hurdles:** For this event, students must capitalize every other letter in a given sentence. The event begins by having students capitalize the first letter of the sentence as they normally would and continues by having them capitalize every other letter in that sentence. This mimics the hurdle event in track and will give your students a real challenge. For example, this is what this line would look like after being typed in the hurdles event:

Type this line. TyPe ThIs LiNe

• **Relay:** All members of the same team line up behind one team member's keyboarding station. The relay begins by having one student type an assigned line. When the first team member completes typing the first line, he stands up to allow the next team member to sit down and type his assigned line. This pattern continues until all students on the team have typed their assigned line. The first team to have all of its members correctly type the lines wins.

The team with the highest score at the end of all events is declared the winner!

Variation: You can have some fun and add realism to the game by using track and field props such as passing a baton for the relay, drawing a track on the board, and using a whistle to start each event.

Materials Needed:
A variety of timed writing paragraphs and sentences.

Time Required:
Teacher's discretion.

Contributor:
Scott Christy, Business Instructor, Green Bay East High School, Green Bay, WI

KEYBOARDING OLYMPICS

Objective:
To provide students with a simulated Olympic type competition that enhances and reinforces speed and accurate keyboarding skills.

Procedure:

You can structure the keyboarding Olympics game as either an individual or team competition.

Here's how to play:

1. Explain to your students that they will be competing against each other (or against other teams) in a keyboarding Olympics competition. The goal is for students to achieve the highest speed and accuracy scores.
2. Conduct timed writing tests.
3. Review the results and determine the gold, silver and bronze medalists.
4. Present your champions with their gold, silver and bronze ribbons or certificates.

You can conduct the keyboarding Olympics several times during a course or as a grand finale to conclude a semester or school year.

Materials Needed:
Timed writing tests, as well as ribbons or alternatively gold, silver, and bronze certificates (available at your local party supply store).

Time Required:
Teacher's discretion depending upon the frequency desired.

Contributor:
JoAnn Novotny, Business Instructor, Longfellow Middle School, Wauwatosa, WI

KEYBOARDING DINOSAUR ENDURANCE

Objective:
To provide students an opportunity to test their endurance in keying lengthy words without hesitating between letters.

Procedure:

The names of various dinosaurs are very long and give students an opportunity to test their endurance in keying lengthy and unfamiliar words without any pauses between keystrokes. The entire alphabet should be taught and practiced before this exercise is used.

Here's how it works:
    Pass out a copy of the list of dinosaurs found on the next page.
    The goal of this activity is for the students to keep their eyes on the screen while typing the dinosaur name. Then, they must follow that word by an <enter> keystroke.
    This is an exercise geared towards speed. Challenge students to complete the greatest number of dinosaur names in two minutes or less.
    You can also find additional names of dinosaurs online at
http://www.cbv.ns.ca/marigold/history/dinosaurs/dinosaurs.html.

Materials Needed:
A list, created by the teacher, of various dinosaurs. A ready-to-reproduce list is included on the next page.

Time Required:
Approximately 10-15 minutes.

Contributor:
Tonya D. Skinner, Business Education Department, Oran High School, Oran, MO. Adapted from the *UltraKey Typing* Web site.

Dinosaur endurance list:

Allosaurus
Apatosaurus
Archaeopteryx
Brachiosaurus
Camptosaurus
Diplodocus
Europlocephalus
Heterodontosaurus
Hipsilophodon
Hypacrosaurus
Herrerasaurus
Ichthyosaurus
Pachycephalosaurus
Parasaurolophus
Planocephalosaurus
Plateosaurus
Procompsognathus
Rhamphorhynchus
Saurolophus
Sauropods
Stegosaurus
Struthiomimus
Tenontosaurus
Triceratops
Tuojiangosaurus
Tyrannosaurus
Velociraptor
Zanclodon

ALPHABETICAL LIST RELAY

Objectives:
To help students improve their composing skills.
To give students practice in using the bulleted list feature found in most word processing software programs.
To challenge students to use critical thinking skills.

Procedure:

Set your clock for a three to five minute timed writing and challenge students to compose an alphabetical list using one of the following categories:

- Items found in a supermarket
- Brand names of items
- Boys' names
- Girls' names
- Cities of the world
- Countries of the world
- Snack foods
- Restaurants

The winner is the student who is the first to complete the alphabetical list. For some categories, a complete alphabetical list may not be possible. If this is the case, then declare the winner as the student who finishes first with the most complete list.

Materials Needed:
A list of topics, (see example provided above), created by the teacher.

Time Required:
Approximately 20-30 minutes.

Contributor:
Tonya D. Skinner, Business Education Department, Oran High School, Oran, MO

STOP THE MUSIC

Objective:
To help sharpen students' ability to think creatively while simultaneously composing work products at the keyboard.

Procedure:

Divide students into equal rows of four or five.
Instruct each student to compose a short story beginning with the same sentence.
Dictate a starter-sentence to your students.
Suggested starter sentences are:

> • The morning headline read…
> • The town was deserted and…
> • It was the night before Christmas and the worst thing that could happen did happen…
> • It was one minute before midnight when we got there and…
> • As the plane left the runway, a strange sound came from the…

At the same time you give the signal to begin, music on a tape or CD should be turned on.

At your discretion, the music should be stopped and each student should move from her machine to the machine next to her in the same row.

When you start the music again, students should continue the story as started by their predecessor. This process continues for as long as you desire, but it is suggested that a minimum of two minutes be given for composing each sentence.

Before the last round, you need to warn the students that the game is ending. They must effectively bring closure to the story that is on the computer in front of them before you stop the music for the last time.

The winning team is the one which, in your opinion, submits the most entertaining and interesting story. It is recommended that the winning story either be posted on a bulletin board or be read aloud to the class.

Formatting rules: Students should have their computer set for double-spacing and understand that since they are composing, format is not important; however, proper spelling and grammar are, so they will be allowed to backspace to make corrections.

Variations: This game can be made more stimulating by requiring a different type of story each time. Possibilities include ghost stories, mystery stories, stories with surprise endings, children's fairy tales, stories with a moral, science fiction, fantasy, and poetry. Most students have a marvelous imagination; with a little encouragement they may create something that will surprise you. You may also wish to have students give the story an appropriate title.

Materials Needed:
Several starter-sentences, designed for maximum creative potential, written on a sheet of paper (see examples provided for suggestions) and a portable CD or cassette player.

Time Required:
Approximately 10-20 minutes depending on the number of times the game is played.

Contributor:
Tonya D. Skinner, Business Education Department, Oran High School, Oran, MO

IDEAS THAT
ACTIVATE &
MOTIVATE

GRAPHING MOTIVATES STUDENTS

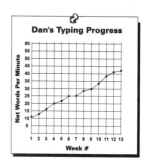

Dan's Typing Progress

Objectives:
To provide a visual image that allows students to:
(a) see their results; (b) gauge their progress; and
(c) motivate them to achieve a higher net words-
per-minute score (NWPM).

Procedure:

Write the name of each student at the top of a sheet of graph paper, one sheet
per student. If anonymity is important then assign each student a code name
or a number.

Moving horizontally across the bottom of the graph paper, students plot
the bottom number line in increments of five. The line begins with the number
five and continues through the number 120 (i.e., 5, 10, 15...120). These
numbers represent the average number of words per minute each student
achieves during timed writings.

The vertical line is the date of the timed typing drills. The bottom point of
this line begins with the earliest date of the timed writings with subsequent
dates added. At the end of each day or week, (as determined by the instructor) each student plots his results on his graph paper by drawing a dot that
corresponds with the week and average NWPM achieved.

Have the students connect the plotted points to form a line graph which
hopefully continues to rise with each new set of timed writings they have
taken.

The typing chart serves as an excellent visual incentive for students to
reach their fullest potential.

Variation: If spatial constraints do not allow you to post graph sheets, have
the students keep and record their own results in a class folder or notebook.

Materials Needed:
One piece of graph paper per student and a large wall or bulletin board.

Time Required:
Use throughout a keyboarding course.

AWARDS AND COMPETITIONS IGNITE
KEYBOARDING ENERGY

Objectives:
To provide incentives that motivate students to excel in class.
To reward students for high achievement in keyboarding skills.

Procedure:

Students appreciate being recognized for high performance. Award certificates, easily generated from a personal computer, provide long-lasting incentives and rewards for the high achieving student.

The following list offers some suggestions along with a graphic image that can be used to create your own personalized certificates:

Statement on Certificate	Graphic Image
Top-notch Typing Award	A happy student typing
A First-Class Keyboarder	A postage stamp
You've Passed the First Speed Bump	A car driving on a road
Your Typing Speed has No Limits	A speedometer
Your Accuracy is Right on Target	A dartboard
Good Typing Posture	A chair

In addition to certificates, hold a regular "type-off" competition. In this game, the students compete against one another in a race to be the fastest and most accurate keyboarder in the class. Award appropriate certificates to the top three finishers.

Materials Needed:
Certificate forms (optional), clipart, computer and printer.

Time Required:
Use throughout a keyboarding course.

59

MAKE YOUR OWN HOME-ROW RULER

Objective:
To create a real-life visual reminder by using old keys from an inoperable or broken keyboard.

Procedure:

Don't throw away those old typewriters or keyboards—recycle them! Remove the "A, S, D, F, J, K, L, ;" keys and glue them to the back of a ruler. Carry your home-row ruler as you walk around the class to constantly remind students of proper finger placement and technique.

You can also make signs on poster boards from the unused letters, such as "Keep your eyes on the copy."

Materials Needed:
Inoperable keyboards and/or typewriters.

Time Required:
Not applicable.

TYPOS CAN BE LIFE-CHANGING

Objective:
To stress the importance of proofreading
documents.

Procedure:

Share the story printed below to illustrate to students, in a humorous manner,
the importance of proofreading.

A businessman from Wisconsin went on a
trip to Louisiana. Upon arrival, he immediately
plugged his laptop into the hotel room
modem connection and sent a short e-mail
back home to his wife, Jennifer Johnson, at
her address, JennJohn@world.net.

Unfortunately, in his hurry, he mistyped one
letter in the address. The e-mail ended up
going to JeanJohn@world.net (Jean
Johnson), in Duluth, the wife of a preacher
who had just been buried that very same day.
The preacher's wife took one look at the e-
mail and fainted. It read, "Arrived safely, but it
sure is hot down here!"

Source: Adapted from "Notes from your chaplain," by
Chaplain Shields Moore.

Materials Needed:
A copy of the story printed above.

Time Required:
5 minutes.

61

WHAT CAN "THIS" BE?

THIS?

Objective:
To reinforce the importance of proofreading to students.

Procedure:

Solving challenging riddles can serve as an effective and fun way to teach. If you're looking for excitement in your keyboarding classes, then you'll love "THIS" idea.

Here's how it works:
    Read the riddle printed on the next page to your students. Offer a prize for the first student who can guess the correct answer. Unless your class is incredibly witty, no one will solve the riddle after hearing it.
    Then, have your students type the riddle and see if they can guess the answer.

Materials Needed:
Copies of the "THIS" riddle (printed on the next page) and small prizes (optional).

Time Required:
Approximately 10 minutes.

Contributor:
Linda Nix, Business Teacher, Mansfield High School, Arlington, TX

The "THIS" Riddle

<u>I</u> can be this, and <u>you</u> can be this. And yes, <u>we</u> can be this. <u>He</u> can't be this, and <u>she</u> can't be this. And no, <u>they</u> can't be this. <u>Dogs</u> can't be this, but <u>cats</u> can. And a <u>kitten</u> can't be this, but a <u>puppy</u> can. <u>Givers</u> can't be this, but <u>beggars</u> can. And <u>humility</u> can't be this, but <u>greed</u> can. Not even <u>peace</u> can be this, but <u>fear</u> can.

What is "this?"

Answer: "This" refers to only those words that can be typed with one hand using the QWERTY typing technique.

USE MAKE-UP SLIPS FOR MAKE-UP WORK

Objective:
To provide the teacher and the student with an effective method of keeping track of missed keyboarding work.

Procedure:

Keeping track of which students owe what work is not one of teaching's greatest joys. An excellent tool for relieving this burden is to use keyboarding make-up slips.

Here's how to use the make-up slips:

When a student is absent, record his name and the current date on a yellow make-up slip.

On the slip, list all the keyboarding drills, new material presented, timed writings and quizzes/tests that were given on that day.

When the absent student returns, simply hand the make-up slip to him.

When the student turns in his make-up work, he must attach the make-up slip to the assignment.

This time saving tool helps you stay organized. Also, it informs the student of the work he missed and the make-up work for which he is responsible.

Materials Needed:
Copies of the "Make-up Slips" (shown on the next page), or one that you create on your own.

Time Required:
Use throughout a keyboarding course.

Contributor:
Diane Heliker, Business Teacher, Battle Creek-Ida Grove High School, Ida Grove, IA

Keyboarding Make-up Slip

Name:_____

Date:_____

Make-up Work

Drills:

New Material:

Timings/Tests:

You must staple this sheet to your make-up work
to receive credit!

THE OVER 30 CLUB

Objective:
To provide students with an incentive to keep improving their average number of words-per-minute.

Procedure:

Take a keyboarding class and turn it into a series of ever more elite clubs. The idea of the *Over 30 Club* is to motivate students to reach higher brackets of typing speeds and to earn "club status" recoginition for doing so.

Here's how to start your *Over 30 Club*:

1. Inform your students that in order to reach the *Over 30 Club*, they must successfully type more than 30 words per minute within an average difficulty 5-minute timing test with no more than 5 errors on two separate occasions. Once this goal is met, the student receives a small prize. *Note: The student receives only one prize for each goal attained.*

2. Once the student has reached the *Over 30 Club,* he moves on to a new goal and attempts to reach the *Over 40 Club*. The criteria for the *Over 40 Club* is the same as the *Over 30 Club,* but the student must key more than 40 words per minute. The *Over 40 Club* members are also rewarded with a prize. Additionally you may opt to have their name(s) read over the school's public announcement system.

3. Let the club levels continue to whatever word-per-minute level your students are capable of achieving.

> A note of caution: watch your budget, it can become quite costly buying prizes. It's best to use inexpensive prizes that increase in value with each new "club" level your students achieve.

Suggested prizes to award:

Club	Prize
Over 30 Club	Candy.
Over 40 Club	Free Day. A student gets to miss a class of his choice with the understanding that it not fall on a day when quizzes or tests are given. Students are allowed to go to the library for the missed period without having to make-up the missed work.
Over 50 Club	A free movie pass.
Over 60 Club	A gift certificate to a music store.
Over 70 Club	Pizza party. A large cheese pizza and bottle of soda is delivered to the recipient and his friends at lunchtime.

Materials Needed:
A variety of small prizes (shown above).

Time Required:
Use throughout a keyboarding course.

Contributor:
Gail Balboni, Business Education Teacher, East Granby High School, East Granby, CT

CHIT-CHAT KEYBOARDING

Objective:
To permit students their natural tendency to
talk to each other during class while
simultaneously having them practice their keyboarding skills.

Procedure:

Take advantage of your students' desire to talk to one another during class by
informing them that they will be participating in an activity that allows them to
chitchat with each other, but not by talking.

Here's how it works:

Have your students pick a partner and allow them to chat with each other
via the computer.

To do this, students use a word processing program and must sit next to
their partner.

Rather than talk to each other, instruct your students to type what they
want to say.

This activity allows you to: (a) maintain a quiet classroom environment; (b)
give students a chance to unleash their gossip needs; and (c) give them good
practice in using their keyboarding skills.

Incorporate this activity into your weekly classroom agenda and you'll
notice a lot less chit-chat among students.

Materials Needed:
No special materials required.

Time Required:
Teacher's discretion.

Contributor:
Robin Hurst, Business Teacher, Fulton High School, Fulton, KY

EVERYONE STARTS TIMED WRITINGS ON TIME

"Your number is 7...and GO"

Objective:
To ensure that all students start timed writing tests at the same time.

Procedure:

"*I haven't said go yet!*" A common phrase spoken by keyboarding teachers in classrooms everywhere. A student starts keying a timed-writing paragraph before the timing clock begins. For the teacher, this situation can be very frustrating in that it slows the entire class down, not to mention the fact that it's not fair game.

Try this simple, yet very effective solution to this old-aged keyboarding classroom problem. Rather than beginning timed writings by saying "ready, set, go" (which tempts students to jump-the-gun and start typing before the word "go" is said), call out a number that students must type a split second before beginning their timed writings.

Example:
Say to your students, "the number of your first timed writing is 7....and go." Students then quickly type the number 7 and begin their timed writing. Wait one second (to give students time to type the number) and then start the timing clock.

Materials Needed:
No special materials required.

Time Required:
Not applicable.

Contributor:
Tammy Block, Business/Computer Teacher, Henry School, Henry, SD

BULLETIN BOARDS
THAT TEACH
KEYBOARDING

STOP, LOOK, AND PROOFREAD

Objective:
To constantly remind students to proofread their work.

Procedure:

To help remind students to consistently proofread their work, make a display that includes a stoplight with the captions "stop," "look" and "proofread" printed on it. The word "stop" is printed in a red circle, "look" is printed in a yellow circle, and "proofread" is printed in a green circle.

The colors represent the familiar colors of traffic stoplights. Red means to stop typing, yellow means to slow down and remember to proofread, and green means to proofread every document before passing it in for grading. To round out the traffic scenario, add proofreader marks and techniques on cutout cars (obtained from a software clipart package). Arrange the stoplight and cars on a bulletin board or poster board in a manner that gives the proofreading scene the appearance of a busy street.

The following list includes common proofreading techniques that can be written on the cutout cars:
- Check for spacing errors
- Check sentence structure
- Check punctuation
- Check spelling
- Check grammar

Materials Needed:
Colored paper, a clipart cutout of automobiles, scissors, and glue.

Time Required:
Not applicable.

Contributor:
Marie Redig, Business Teacher, Southeast Polk High School, Runnells, IA

GET CAUGHT POSING WITH PERFECT TECHNIQUE

Objective:
To provide a visual reinforcement stressing the need for students to adhere to proper keyboarding techniques and to use good typing posture.

Procedure:

"Get Caught Posing With Perfect Technique" is the headline for this energizing keyboarding bulletin board idea. This excellent visual tool is easy to construct and makes a great display for an open house or parents' night.

Here's how it works:

To build the board, cut from construction paper white squares and small triangle black picture placeholders. Glue the edges of the black triangle to the corners of the white squares.

On each "picture square," write one form of proper keyboarding technique that the students are required to master (e.g., "keep your eyes on your textbook").

Place the picture squares randomly on a bulletin board.

As a student masters a proper technique and begins applying it consistently on a daily basis, take her picture using a Polaroid® or digital camera and add it to the bulletin board or wall.

The "Get Caught Posing With Perfect Technique" bulletin board emphasizes one of the first and most important steps students need to master in a keyboarding course. It's also an effective visual aid to which students can refer. Students will love seeing their pictures on the bulletin board and will be proud of their accomplishment.

The students not yet pictured can visually see someone using proper technique and in turn will be motivated to accomplish the goal and have their pictures added to the board.

Material Needed:
Construction paper, scissors, glue, a Polaroid® or digital camera, a marker and a bulletin board or wall space.

Time Required:
Ongoing, use throughout a keyboarding course

Contributor:
Kimberly Greenlee, Business Teacher, Cranberry Area Jr.-Sr. High School, Seneca, PA

MASTER THE MILES!

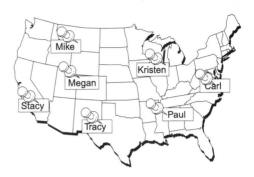

Objectives:
To provide students with an achievement incentive to improve their typing speed and accuracy. To provide a fun way to expand on the students knowledge of United States geography.

Procedure:

Convert timed writing scores into mileage and let your students travel the United States.

Here's how it works:

1. Place a large, detailed map of the United States in your classroom.
2. Give each student a tack and a small slip of paper with her name on it.
3. Place a tack on the map where your school is located.
4. Have each student choose a destination on the map that she wants to reach and have her mark that spot by tacking her paper to the selected area on the map.
5. Calculate the miles from your school to the student's destination and convert timed writing scores into miles. Students will now travel to their destination. For example, a 30 words-per-minute timed writing is equal to 10 miles. Create your own words-per-minute to miles conversion chart based on the skill level of your students.
6. Have the students keep a travel log telling about the cities, sites, weather, etc. Encorage them to access the Internet and/or travel books to gather this information. Additionally, have students share their travel experiences that occur along the way.
7. Establish a deadline, such as the end of a marking period, for students to reach their destination.

Materials Needed:

A detailed map of the United States of America, pushpins, small slips of paper with each student's name written or typed on it, and a corkboard.

Time Required:

Use throughout a keyboarding or typing course.

Contributor:

Donna J. Birkby, Business & Technology Teacher, Avon Lake High School, Avon Lake, OH

CREATING A LIFE-SIZE KEYBOARD DISPLAY

Objective:
To create a large, visually stimulating keyboarding display that enhances the overall classroom environment.

Procedure:

Is your keyboarding chart large enough for students to see? Is it big enough for you to make easy reference to when introducing new keys to students? Here's an inexpensive idea to make a very large keyboard display for your classroom.

Here's how to make the display:
Obtain some small aluminum foil sheet trays to represent the different keys. (Hint: ask your local supermarket if it will donate some for your project).
Using a word processing or desktop publishing program, print each letter and/or symbol that you want to include in your display. Be sure that the size is approximately equivalent to the size of the meat trays. Cut the letter and/or symbols along their outlines. Laminate each one (optional) and glue them to the individual meat trays.
Next, using poster board, attach two long pieces of styrofoam in a parallel fashion (see the illustration shown below). Using pushpins or glue, attach the sheet trays to the stryrofoam in the QWERTY keyboard style.
Mount the keyboard to your wall. You now have a life-size keyboard for easy teacher and student reference.

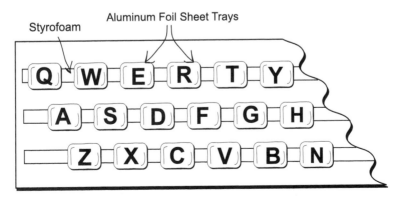

Materials Needed:

Aluminum foil sheet trays, a computer, a printer, a lamination machine (optional), poster board, styrofoam and pushpins or glue.

Time Required:

Not applicable.

Contributor:

Angie Palmer, Computer/Vocational Education Teacher,
Brown Middle School, Thomasville, NC

LET IT SNOW, LET IT SNOW, LET IT SNOW

Objective:
To provide students with a visual incentive to improve typing speed and accuracy.

Procedure:

During the winter months, try this wonderful idea of having your students build a snowman, flake-by-flake. It's a very "cool" idea to motivate your students to type faster.

Here's how it works:

After students have learned all of the alphabetic keys and have had several practices with timed writings, spend one day setting typing speeds. The students do this by typing one-minute paragraph timed writings, then selecting their best speed of the day.

After the students leave the class, use masking tape to outline a huge snowman on one of the walls of your classroom.

The following day explain to the students that when the class works on speed development (as opposed to accuracy) they will be able to put a snowflake on the wall with their name on it each time they beat their previous high speed.

Once a snowflake is posted, the increased speed becomes the number they must exceed in order to put another snowflake on the wall. Snowflakes can be made out of simple cutouts or you can use your school's die cut machine.

When the activity first begins, students quickly increase their speed and a lot of snowflakes are put on the wall to fill out the snowman. However, it soon becomes more difficult to increase speed, and it becomes a real honor to be able to add a snowflake to the snowman. Your students will find this a fun and challenging activity.

Variation: This activity can easily be adapted to the time of the year that your particular class begins working on speed development. You could mask out the outline of an apple, a butterfly, a heart, or whatever your imagination will allow.

Materials Needed:

Masking tape, and cutouts of paper snowflakes.

Time Required:

Use throughout a keyboarding course.

Contributor:

Sandi Bullington, Business Teacher, Neosho School, Neosho, MO

"AROUND THE WORLD IN KEYBOARDING" PROGRAM

Objectives:
To enhance students' typing, reading, and spelling abilities.
Can also be used as a supplemental exercise when students complete their assigned work early.

Procedure:

A student's typing speed is often tied to her reading and spelling abilities. In order to address this issue and provide additional enrichment to the curriculum, have your students participate in the "Around the World in Keyboarding" program.

Here's how it works:

1. Prepare a typed paragraph in each of the following languages: English, Spanish, French, German, Italian and Japanese. The Web site FreeTranslation.com (**www.freetranslation.com**) can assist you in accomplishing this task in just a few minutes. Additionally, use an online encyclopedia to research which countries use these languages as their official language.

2. Post a list of the languages and the corresponding countries (i.e., list all the countries that use Spanish as their official languge) next to a large world poster on your classroom wall.

3. Explain to the students that they will start their journey in the United States and will type the first paragraph in English. A "hot-air balloon" is taped over the United States on the map with the word "start" written on it.

4. Students then begin visiting countries of their choice and typing the paragraph in the appropriate language. They must visit a country that speaks each listed language before they can repeat any language. Students may visit an English speaking country only once in a class period. (Spanish-speaking students are encouraged to visit a Spanish-speaking country only once during a class period.) Each paragraph must be labeled with the student's name, the country she is visiting, and the official language of the country.

5. At the end of the day, cut out each paragraph and tape it to the back of the "hot-air balloon."

81

Materials Needed:

One paragraph of text typed in the following languages: English, Spanish, French, German, Italian and Japanese.

Time Required:

Teacher's discretion.

Contributor:

Sandi Bullington, Business Teacher, Neosho School, Neosho, MO

"FAST TRACK" KEYBOARDING EXCITEMENT

Objective:

To encourage students to reach their fullest typing potential.

Procedure:

To encourage keyboarding students to reach for top typing speeds, put a large racecar track on your classroom wall. This is a creative motivator that will surely improve keyboarding skills and add some "fast track" excitement to your keyboarding classroom.

Here's how it works:

1. On a poster board or bulletin board, designate a starting point and label it the "pit-stop area." Label the four turns of the "track" with words-per-minute ranges. Every student begins at the starting pit-stop area, which is labeled "under 20 wpm." Each

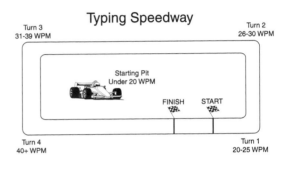

additional pit-stop is located at various corners on the racetrack and designated using higher words-per-minute in progression on the track. Turn One is labeled 20-25 wpm; Turn Two is labeled 26-30 wpm; Turn Three is labeled 31-35 wpm; and Turn Four is labeled 40 wpm or higher. Adjust the wpm ranges according to the skill of your students.

2. Each student is required to cut out a picture of a racecar (or any car of his choice) from a magazine and write his name on the back of the picture.

3. Apply sticky tape to the back of the cars causing them to adhere to the racetrack.

4. Initially, all the cars are placed in the starting pit area and must remain there until a student reaches a speed of 20 wpm on a three minute timed writing (or whatever time you deem appropriate).

5. As the number of words-per-minute increases, students advance their cars toward turns 1, 2, 3 and 4.

Variation: Add realism to the racing theme by decorating the wall with checkered flags and racing posters.

Materials Needed:
A bulletin or poster board decorated like the illustration provided.

Time Required:
Use throughout a keyboarding course.

Contributor:
Laura Hazelett, Business Education Teacher, South Point High School, South Point, OH

HANDS-OFF WITH MAGNETIC KEYS

Objectives:
To provide students with a visual reinforcement of the letter keys.
To relieve boredom by allowing students to take a break from their keyboarding workstations.

Procedure:

There are times when your students need a break from keying. When you sense this need amongst your students, try this "hands-off" reinforcement technique.

Have students go to a designated whiteboard in your classroom where the magnetic letters are randomly mixed.

Challenge your students to arrange the letters and symbols (if desired), in QWERTY keyboard layout order.

You can even time each student to add a touch of competitiveness to the activity.

How to make the letters:
You will need to purchase self-adhesive business card magnets (available at most office product supply stores). Using a word processing software application, type each letter and symbol found on a standard keyboard. Change the font size to about 28 points and print the document. Cut the letters out and affix them to the self-adhesive business card magnets. An easier alternative is to purchase a set of colored children's alphabet magnets.

Materials Needed:
Self-adhesive business card magnets, all twenty-six letters of the alphabet printed out individually and a whiteboard.

Time Required:
Can be used at various times throughout a keyboarding course.

Contributor:
Sheila Miller, Business Teacher, Newfound Regional High School, Bristol, NH

THE KEYBOARDING WALL OF FAME

Objective:

To recognize the fastest keyboarders in your school.

Procedure:

To inspire and ignite enthusiasm year-after-year, build a keyboarding wall of fame. It is an excellent tool that allows you to recognize, over time, the outstanding achievers in your class.

Here's how it works:

Choose an area of your classroom that will be the designated wall of fame spot.

Complete the wall of fame using the following informaiton for each keyboarding recipient added to the wall:

- The top ten number of words per minute scores.
- The respecitve students' names.
- The year the scores were recorded.

At the end of each year, update your record book (used to record keyboarding timing scores) and update the keyboarding wall of fame.

Our contributor, Julie Warnemunde, says "students try to knock-off former students and friends; graduates, especailly siblings, come back to see for themselves if their name is still on the wall."

Materials Needed:

An empty spot on one of your classroom wall's or a large poster board.

Time Required:

An ongoing activity that continues from year-to-year.

Contributor:

Julie Warnemunde, Keyboarding/Business Instructor, Norfolk Junior High School, Norfolk, NE

DRILL & PRACTICE
ACTIVITIES

TYPE IT BACKWARDS

"Z Y X W ..."

Objectives:
To add variety to a keyboarding class.
To improve keystroke accuracy.

Procedure:

Avoiding monotony in a keyboarding class is always a challenge. To infuse variety into the class while promoting accuracy, have your students type the alphabet backwards.

Here's how it works:

Begin the activity by having the students focus their eyes on a fixed point somewhere in front of them (e.g., the corner, a poster on the wall, etc.). Do not let students look down at their keyboards or typewriters. Focusing on something other than the teachers face will reduce mental distractions and allow the students to visualize the keyboard in their minds. The students should be challenged to achieve 100 percent accuracy.

Once the students have confirmed their readiness, begin dictating the alphabet backwards. Adjust the speed of the dictation according to the skill level of the class.

At the conclusion of each dictation session, provide verbal motivators such as "great accuracy" and "nice work" to the top achievers.

Materials Needed:
No special materials required.

Time Required:
Approximately ten minutes.

Contributor:
Geraldine Newlon, Business Educator, Liberty High School, Clarksburg, WV

NAME YOUR DICTATION DRILLS

"aaa *space* afa *space* JASON *space* jaj ..."

Objectives:
To add variety to dictation drills.
To publicly recognize the students in your classroom by their first name.

Procedure:

Communicate to your students that they should inform you when they have learned enough letters to spell out their first names. Keep a written list of these names on a sheet of paper that is easily accessible to you during keyboarding dictation drill exercises.

Prior to dictation practice, chose a name from the list that reinforces the keys being learned. During the dictation drill, sporadically state the student's name interspersed with the letters of the drill. Example dictation: "aaa space Tom space fff space…"

Your students will smile a little brighter when they hear their name being called out loud and you'll see them perk up as the entire class is typing their name during dictation drills.

Materials Needed:
None.

Time Required:
Not applicable.

Contributor:
Teresa Boulds, Business Instructor, Eldorado High School, Eldorado, IL

DRILL & PRACTICE USING SPRINTS

Objective:
To improve typing speed by using quick and short bursts of finger energy.

Procedure:

It's an oldie but a goodie—the keyboarding sprint. Keyboarding sprints allow students to exercise their keyboarding muscles by engaging in drills that use short bursts of keying strokes.

Here's how it works:

1. Obtain the appropriate typing text materials and distribute them to your students.

2. Explain the exercise to the students by drawing the analogy that keyboarding sprints for a keyboarding student are like running sprints for a track and field athlete. Sprints are performed in short bursts to maximize a runner's speed and conditioning skills. Instruct your students to focus on speed and accuracy.

3. Start by setting your timer or hand-held watch to thirty seconds. Begin the first drill. Continue to do five drills at 30 seconds each. Tell the students not to go back and correct their mistakes. The goal is to type as quickly and accurately as possible in the given timeframe.

4. Cut the time to 20 seconds and do five drills. Then do five drills each lasting 15 seconds, 10 seconds and finally 5 seconds in length.

Materials Needed:
Typing drill sentences and a stop watch.

Time Required:
Teacher's discretion. Usually ten minutes is adequate for the sprint drills to be effective.

TYPING TONGUE TWISTERS

Objective:
To reinforce new letters that are introduced to
your students.

Procedure:

A simple yet effective mechanism for reinforcing new letter keys that are being
introduced is to have students think of tongue twister sentences that include
and repeat the new letters being learned.

Here's an example if the letter "W" is being introduced:
Wanda walked willingly to work on Wednesday.

Build a collection of the best tongue twisters to use in future lessons.

Note: Tongue twisters can also be used for a daily warm-up keying exercise.

Materials Needed:
No special materials required.

Time Required:
Approximately 4-5 minutes.

Contributor:
Tory Klementsen, MCP, Business and Technology Educator,
Marysville Pilchuck High School, Marysville, WA

93

POSTURE, TECHNIQUE & FINGER PLACEMENT ACTIVITIES

A REAL HANDS-ON QUIZ

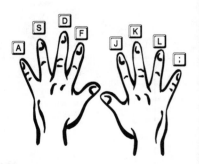

Objective:
To test students proper finger placement
knowledge after they have learned a set
number of letter and/or symbol keys.

Procedure:

Depending on the number of keys introduced to your keyboarding class,
students trace their left and right hand on a sheet of paper and write the
corresponding letters given on the proper fingers used to strike that key.
Students are not allowed to look at a keyboard while taking the quiz.

A sample quiz, to use as a guideline to create your own, is provided on the
next page.

Suggestion: Create a new quiz at the end of each week or timeframe when
new keys are introduced.

Materials Needed:
Copies of the quiz shown on the next page or one that you create on your
own.

Time Required:
Approximately 10-15 minutes.

Contributor:
Renee Holloway, Business Teacher, North High School, North St. Paul, MN

Hands-on Keyboarding Quiz

Name:_____

INSTRUCTIONS: Trace your left and right hand in the space provided below. Write the letter or letters given below above the finger that is used to type each letter.

LETTERS:

DKGOTPV
NBGCVEX

Trace your left and right hand inside this box.

WHERE ARE THE DOTS ON THE "F" AND "J" KEYS?

Objective:
To help students properly place their hands on the home-row keys.

Procedure:

Many students cannot feel the "dots" on the F and J keys on the keyboard— an important feature of the keyboard which allows a user to find the home row keys without looking. Adding to the difficulty, there are some keyboards 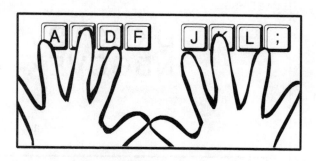 that do not provide any method of finding the home position.

After noticing this problem in her computer lab, our contributor Ellen Paxton, began using self-stick Velcro cut into one-quarter inch squares to help students locate keys without the need to look down. "It's a real time saver and effective method in teaching students not to look at their keys," Paxton says.

Materials Needed:
Self-stick Velcro strips.

Time Required:
Not applicable.

Contributor:
Ellen Paxton, Business Coordinator, Armstrong High School, Plymouth, MN

PAPERCLIPS, BELLS, AND ERASERS, OH MY

Objective:
To demonstrate the importance of not looking at the keys while typing.

Procedure:

This activity employs a terrific technique in teaching keyboarding students the importance of not looking at their keys while typing.

Here's how it works:

At the beginning of the school year, fill a bag with common items such as a paperclip, a rubber band, a pencil, an eraser, a bell and a key. Don't let your students know what you've put in the bag.

Then have each student come to the front of the classroom and put her hand in the bag to "touch" the items without looking at them.

Upon returning to their desks the students make a list of the items they "touched" in the bag.

Variation: Allow students to return to the paper bag for repeated guesses. At the conclusion of the activity, draw the parallel for your students that while looking in the bag would allow them to easily identify the objects (the same principle as looking down at the keys allows them to easily identify the keys) it won't teach them to use their other senses.

The more frequently the students reach into the bag the better they are able to correctly name the objects. This activity stresses the importance of practice and self-discipline.

Materials Needed:
A paper bag, a paperclip, a rubber band, a pencil, an eraser, a bell and a key.

Time Required:
Approximately 20 minutes depending on the number of students that participate in the demonstration.

Contributor:
Lisa Overby, Business/Computer Education Teacher,
Tishomingo County High School, Iuka, MS

CLIPART EYES KEEP STUDENTS LOOKING AT TEXT

KEEP YOUR EYES ON THE COPY

Objective:
To provide a constant visual reminder to encourage students to not look at their keyboards while typing.

Procedure:

Try this quick tip to help students keep their eyes on the text they are typing and not on their keys.

Print out a graphic image of an eye using a software clipart package. Make one copy of the eye for each typing station in your classroom. Cut out the eyes and tape them to the typing stands (the side that faces the student) at each workstation.

You'll notice your students focusing more on the *eye* rather than on their keys.

Materials Needed:
Cutouts of clipart eyes.

Time Required:
Not applicable.

POLISH YOUR KEYS AND STUDENTS WON'T LOOK

Objective:
To force students to not look at their keys while typing.

Procedure:

Dab a small amount of colored fingernail polish on each key (enough to cover each letter) on your keyboards. Let the fingernail polish dry.

Since your students will not be able to read each key, they'll be forced to learn the keyboard by touch.

The fingernail polish can be easily removed using a small amount of fingernail polish remover. You may wish to test this technique on an old keyboard before applying the nail polish to your regularly used keyboards.

Note: Check with your technology coordinator or the person in charge of computer hardware to get approval before applying fingernail polish to the keyboards.

Materials Needed:
A bottle of fingernail polish.

Time Required:
Not applicable.

Contributor:
Kim Hobbs, Business Teacher, Lakewood High School, Salemburg, NC

SERVE-UP SOME SCRAMBLED KEYS

Objective:
To give students practice in memorizing proper
finger placement on the keyboard. Note: Use
only after all letters of the alphabet have been
introduced.

Procedure:

Bad habits are hard to break. Use this idea to ensure that students will never
develop the bad habit of looking down at their keys.

Here's how it works:

Using a small flathead screwdriver, carefully pop off the top row of letter
keys on all of the keyboards in your classroom.

Put each letter key back on the keyboards—the secret here is to place
each key in a different location from its original placement.

Repeat this process for both the middle and bottom letter rows. Leave the
"F" and "J" keys in their original position to provide students with an anchor
position for the home-row location.

Now your students have no choice—they have to learn proper finger
placement in order to type.

Note: Before scrambling the keys, be sure to get the approval of other
teachers, if any, that share your classroom.

Materials Needed:
A small flathead screwdriver.

Time Required:
Use throughout a keyboarding course.

Contributor:
Debbie Graven, Business Teacher, Pleasant Plains High School,
Pleasant Plains, IL

TYPE WITH BOXER SHORTS

Objective:
To force students to not look at their keys
or fingers while they are typing.

Procedure:

To encourage students to learn good touch keying and to not look at their
fingers, try using boxer shorts.

Here's how it works:

Ask each student in your class to bring in a pair of boxer shorts.

Instruct your students to put their keyboards through the elastic part of the
boxer shorts so that the legs of the shorts are facing the student.

Next, have the students place their hands through the legs of boxer shorts
and position their fingers correctly on the home row keys.

This technique really gets students concentrating on their sense of touch.

Materials Needed:
One pair of boxer shorts per student.

Time Required:
Use throughout a keyboarding course

Contributor:
Bruce Baker, Business Education Teacher, Kempsville High School,
Virginia Beach, VA

BONUS SECTION:

KEYBOARDING & TYPING INTERNET RESOURCE DIRECTORY

A note to the reader: The accuracy of each Web site address was verified at the time this book was published. Due to frequent changes, some Web site addresses may no longer be accurate or active. If this is the case, try using an Internet search engine to find the indicated site.

100 Most Common Typing Mistakes

Here are the 100 most frequently misspelled words by typists using the
standard 'qwerty' keyboard and the Dvorak keyboard.
http://web.mit.edu/jcb/www/Dvorak/demons.html

Accu-Type

Full typing course software. Offers a free trial to download.
http://www.learntotype.com/index.htm

All the Right Type Software

Lab pack based software offering a host of features to keep keyboarders
motivated while learning how to type. Includes interactive typing games,
customizable screens, lessons, progress tracker and more! Free software
demo to download.
http://www.ingenuityworks.com/iworks/main

Browser Based Timer for Timing Tests

If you ever lose your manual timer, here's a quick solution. Go online and use
a Web based online timer for timing tests. Just enter the desired timing test
length and hit "start."
http://www.teachnet.com/powertools/neattools/timer/index.html

Captain Keyboard

Space invaders style game that reinforces typing skills by flashing words on
screen that must be typed correctly to progress to more difficult levels.
http://www.zoogma.com/main.htm

Computer Circus

A Web site developed by *Thinkquest* that provides practice in learning the
keyboard.
http://library.thinkquest.org/18709/data/contents.html

Data Entry Keystroke Test Software

This program measures your keyboarding skills, keystrokes per hour, and accuracy. There are three test types: numeric, alpha, and alphanumeric. You can create new, randomly generated tests at any time. Offers a free 30-day software trial.
http://www.testedokonline.com

Disney's Online Timon & Pumbaa Typing Game

Online interactive typing game that challenges students speed and accuracy. Good to use for the student that finishes her assignments early.
http://disney.go.com/DisneyInteractive/flash/index.html?23

Downloadable Proofreader's Marks

Download a handy reference guide of proofreader's marks for the keyboarding teacher and student.
http://www.espressographics.com/text/proofreader.html

EasyType

Offers a free online typing course and testing center. A great resource for any keyboarding teacher!
http://easytype.com

Elite Typing Software

Free download of *EliteTyping* software.
http://www.clasys.com

FasType Typing Tutor

Offers a free trial download of a typing tutorial software.
http://www.trendtech.com

Flash Typing

Offers interactive individualized instruction software on learning how to type. An online demo is available at the Web site.
http://www.flashtyping.com/main.html

107

FREE Typing Games
TypingMaster Games is a free package of three challenging typing games that have been designed for typists to improve their typing speed and reactivity as well as cut down on errors.
http://www.typingmaster.com

History of Typewriters
Read all about the evolution of the modern day typewriter.
http://xavier.xu.edu/~polt/tw-history.html

Hit the Dots Mouse Game
Click on the radio buttons as they are selected randomly by the computer. This game helps develop skills controlling the mouse.
http://members.inter-linc.net/users/alwims/Hit_The_Dot.html

Keyboarding Bingo
The makers of *Mavis Beacon Teaches Typing* software include a full description of how to play a keyboarding bingo game.
http://www.mavisbeacon.com/teachers_lounge.html

Keyboarding Online
This teacher created Web site contains a host of online tools and goodies for the keyboarding teacher. Features include posture and technique guidelines, handouts, rubrics and scores of useful links.
http://www.crews.org/curriculum/ex/compsci/keyboarding/index.htm

Keyboarding Puzzles
Interactive Web site that challenges visitors to drag and drop pieces of a keyboard puzzle.
http://www.davis.k12.ut.us/etc/paul/sample/Keyboard/index.htm

Keyboarding Support Center
The makers of *UltraKey* keyboarding software provide site visitors with lots
of activities and tips on teaching keyboarding.
http://www.bytesoflearning.com/UltraKey/KeyHomeT.htm

Keyboarding Teaching Tips
This site contains an organizational method of how to introduce keyboarding
or typing to students. Helpful graphics are included.
http://belnet.bellevue.k12.wa.us/class/curr.pgs/wp/kybdg.html

Keyboarding Technique Adventure
This site contains a variety of links relating to proper typing technique, posture
and ergonomics.
http://www.oasd.k12.wi.us/Schools/Parklawn/keyboarding.htm

Keyboarding Template
Download and print a keyboarding template.
http://www.teachnet.com/lesson/tech/keyboarding110900.html

Keyboarding with the Keyboard Coach
A tutorial software that provides a step-by-step teaching medium for teacher
and student to work together or independently. Free trial demo software
available.
http://www.thelearningstudio.com/keyboarding1.html

Learn 2 Type
Master the skills of typing using the interactive online exercises that adjust to
your skill.
http://www.learn2type.com

Learning Posture for Keyboarding
Contains a variety of reasons to practice proper posture while typing.
http://www.bytesoflearning.com/UltraKey/Posture/Posture.htm

Letter Chase Typing Tutor Software
This site offers a free download version of a complete typing program for all levels.
http://www.letterchase.com

NimbleFingers Software
Offers a free download of an easy-to-use touch typing software, a keyboarding fable and some keyboarding teaching ideas.
http://www.nimblefingers.com

Proven Techniques for Teaching QWERTY Keyboarding
A computer teacher offers a host of good tips and strategies to implement in keyboarding classrooms.
http://www.cwu.edu/~setc/ldtech/keyboarding_techniques.html

QWERTY Connection
Offers a brief description about the history of typing, typewriters, and the QWERTY technique. Some good information to use with beginning typists.
http://home.earthlink.net/~dcrehr/

Spacing and Punctuation Rules
This Web site contains many useful spacing and punctuation rules for word processing documents.
http://www.mtdaily.com/style.html

Stress Reduction & Break Time Activities
Try some stress reduction and break time keyboarding activities that keep the body limber and your fingers nimble.
http://www.nimblefingers.com/a_exer.htm

SuperKids Educational Reviews
Parent, teacher, and student teams' comparison of nine typing programs.
http://www.superkids.com/aweb/pages/reviews/typing1/sw_sum1.shtml

Teaching Keyboarding — When? Why? How?
An "everything you ever wanted to know" article on why teaching and learning keyboarding is the number one computer skill to possess.
http://www.education-world.com/a_tech/tech072.shtml

Tonya Skinner's Keyboarding Lessons and Ideas
This business education teacher and contributor to this book, has created a wonderful Web site offering plenty of lesson ideas and activities as well as a variety of keyboarding links.
http://www.angelfire.com/ks/tonyaskinner/keybrd.html

Type Right Software
Type Right software teaches students correct hand placement, precision, and speed the old fashioned way.
http://www.geocities.com/typerightsoftware/

Typin's Cool Learning System
A teacher-led, video-based training system that provides a simple "road map" to the keyboard.
http://www.typins-cool.com

TypingTutors.com
Lists the best typing software under a variety of categories.
http://www.typingtutors.com

Typing Injury Frequently Asked Questions (FAQ)
The Typing Injury FAQ (frequently asked questions) is an educational site, provided by the CTD Resource Network, Inc., containing a wide variety of information about repetitive strain injuries, resources for dealing with these ailments, and a broad description of products to reduce keyboarding injury risk and symptoms.
http://www.tifaq.com/index.html

111

Typing Test Online
This site allows users to select a skill level and enter text as it is displayed on screen. Click the "done" button and a dialog box reports the time, accuracy, and the average number of words per minute achieved.
http://www.coolbreeze.co.uk/guide/games/typing%20test/

Typing Tests Online
Offers Web based typing tests. Also offers testing in office skills and numeric keypad categories.
http://www.typing-test.com/index.html

Typing Pal Online
Offers a full typing course online and a free typing test evaluation.
http://www.typingpal.com

Typing Posture Guidelines
The 3M Corporation provides an excellent Web page that can be printed and used as a handout to give to students to stress the importance of using good posture while typing.
**http://www.mmm.com/market/omc/om_html/cws_html/selfhelp/
posture.html**

Typing Rubric Maker
Everything you need to make and print your own customized typing rubric. Just fill in your school name, rubric title, your name, number of words per minute that defines a mastery score, choose a graphic and voila...a printable typing rubric chart appears on screen ready to print.
http://teachers.teach-nology.com/web_tools/rubrics/keyboard/

Typing Technique Checklist
Nifty checklist that highlights all the important elements of proper typing position, posture and technique.
http://www.sasked.gov.sk.ca/docs/elemkey/technique.html

UltraKey Keyboarding Software Trial
Download a free trial version of *UltraKey* keyboarding software. UltraKey 4.0 takes keyboarding instruction into the 21st century with stunning 3-D multimedia and voice accompanied instruction, coupled with a friendly and incredibly comprehensive learning management system.
http://www.bytesoflearning.com/Sales/trials.html

What is the Dvorak Keyboard?
The Dvorak keyboard layout is argued to be a vastly more comfortable and efficient alternative to the standard 'QWERTY' pattern. Learn more about the Dvorak keyboard at this Web site.
http://www.mwbrooks.com/dvorak/index.html

Workstation Ergonomics
This Web site provides excellent guidelines for workstation ergonomics including good posture, workstation design elements, the work environment, stretching exercises, additional Web sites on ergonomics and a self-evaluation checklist.
http://www.ithaca.edu/safety/ergonomics/index.htm

World's Fastest Typist
Read how Mrs. Barbara Blackburn of Salem, Oregon maintains 150 words-per-minute for 50 minutes as recorded in *The Guinness Book of World Records*.
http://sominfo.syr.edu/facstaff/dvorak/blackburn.html

Try
TEACHING
BUSINESS EDUCATION
NEWSLETTER

FREE

Try the number one teaching idea resource for business educators FREE! Just reply to this offer and your FREE issue of Teaching Business Education Newsletter will be shipped to you immediately.

Two ways to start your FREE trial subscription:

1. Online at **www.teachbused.com**
2. Fill out and mail or fax the form below.

 **YES!** Start my FREE trial subscription to TEACHING BUSINESS EDUCATION NEWSLETTER

I understand that I will receive my first issue FREE with no obligation. When I receive the invoice, I will either pay the subscription amount or return it marked "cancel" and owe nothing. The first issue is mine to keep at no charge.

NAME: _____

TITLE: _____

SCHOOL: _____

ADDRESS: _____

CITY: _____

STATE: _____ ZIP: _____

MAIL OR FAX THIS
FORM TO:
TBE NEWSLETTER
BOX 8558,
WARWICK, RI 02888
FAX: 401-781-7608

Get Your Keyboarding Ideas Published in Teaching Business Education Newsletter's Next Book...

COMING SOON!

TEACHING BusinessEducation™
N E W S L E T T E R

More **Games Keyboarding Teachers Play**

Get national recognition for your keyboarding teaching wizardry!

HOW TO GET YOUR IDEA PUBLISHED:

Following the format used in this book, send your best keyboarding or typing game, lesson, activitiy, or project using any of the following methods below:

1. E-mail your idea to: **contact@teachbused-email.com**. Please put "MGKTP IDEA SUBMISSION" in the subject line.
2. Fax your idea to: **1-401-781-7608**.
3. Mail your idea to: **Teaching Business Education Newsletter, Box 8558, Warwick, RI 02888**.
4. Visit our Web site at **www.teachbused.com** and click on the "Get Published" button.

Be sure to include your name, job title, and school or home address (as you would like them to appear in the book) with each submission.